T0365336

ISBN: 978-1-4907-5394-2 (sc)
        978-1-4907-5393-5 (e)

Library of Congress Control Number: 2015900741

Trafford rev. 01/22/2015

 www.trafford.com

North America & international
toll-free: 1 888 232 4444 (USA & Canada)
fax: 812 355 4082

I
HATE
SIN

Obioma Okerekeugo

DEDICATION

I dedicate this book, *I Hate Sin*, to the memory of my late father, Dr. Ijeoma Joseph Ogbonna Okerekeugo, a renowned physician who brought joy, peace, and harmony to my wonderful mother, to me, and the rest of my brothers and sisters and to the world at large. Whomever he touches, his shadow of light and love turns their darkness into light.

And also to the memory of my beloved younger brother, Ndubuizu lhechukwu Okerekeugo, a brave man and spokesman for the family. When he was around, enemies didn't intrude against the family without a righteous reprimand filled with love and a gentle spirit.

May your gentle spirit and that of our dad rest in perfect peace till we meet, not to part anymore.

I also dedicate this book to my late beloved mother, Mrs. Helen Ngozi Okerekeugo, a tigress so to say, filled with compassion and love that she exemplified to me and the rest of the family. Wisdom and the fear of God are her anchors, and that is why she led all of us to Jesus Christ of Nazareth.

To Nnanyelugo and Goodluck, my beautiful, loving brothers.

To Adanma and Onyinyechukwu, my beautiful, loving sisters, and their children.

To my loving and beautiful wife, Lovelyn Okerekeugo.

To my childhood friends, Emmanuel Agu, Brother Emmanuel Ejei, Ifeanyi Ejiofor, Christian Nnoli, Emeka Anyaegbuna, and John Ofor (of blessed memory). Blessings to all of you.

"*The wages of sin is death; but the gift of God is eternal life through Jesus Christ of Nazareth*" (*Romans* 6:23).

Sin opens us up to the attack of the enemy (*the devil*).

CONTENTS

ACKNOWLEDGMENTS

Lovelyn Okerekeugo

To my loving and beautiful wife, thank you for your consistent prayers for me and my family. God bless you.

To my aunties, Adeline, Mercy, Blessing, Comfort, Florence, Udu maga, and Dina.

Grandmama and Aunt Harried Udempi Okoronkwo.

Uncles Papa Chukwuemeka (of blessed memory), Papa Ezuma (o.b.m.), Omeruo, Ezikpe, and Chikezie.

Cousins Okechukwu, Ugwuokoro, Ogbonnie, and Udobi.

Friends Brother Paul Malone, Jeff Bosakawski, Pastor Arthur McColum (o.b.m.), Pastor Flavio, Bishop Bob Jackson, and Pastor Rasaki.

Nieces Chibuzo and Chidiogo.

PREVIEW

The scripture, the Word of God, stipulates that man had a union with God and was in great harmony with him until man disobeyed God by giving heed to Lucifer, who disguised himself as a serpent. (Genesis 1:26–31, 3).

The Word of God states that as a result, sin entered into the world. And subsequently, because God hated sin so much, he judged sin in the cross of Calvary. Death, sickness, disease, disappointment, and war and confusion entered the world. And man became a slave to sin and the devil. (Romans 6:22–23; John 10:10).

According to the truth of the Word of God, the first family was Adam and Eve, and God gave them a simple command. And the command was, "out of all the trees in the garden, thou shall not eat of the tree of the knowledge of good and evil. The day that you shall eat of it, thou shall surely die." And man was deceived by the deceiver, murderer, liar, thief, and the eternal oppressor. Upon that deceit, man fell from grace and fellowship with God and lost his dominion to Lucifer and his demons, which are fallen angels that disobeyed God.

Sin will finally be eradicated when Christ Jesus of Nazareth will return physically to take those who believe in his atoning work on the cross of Calvary. And those who do not believe will be cast into the lake that burns with fire and brimstone that was initially prepared for the devil and his demons and those that did not receive Christ. It is inescapable. No human being born from Adam into this planet can escape these two processes: heaven or hell. My prayer is that I and you will make heaven. Apostle Paul wrote by the inspiration of the Holy Spirit in 2 Corinthians 5:ll, "Knowing therefore the terror of the Lord, we persuade men. Why? Because "nothing that defileth shall enter that city."

As you read this book, *I Hate Sin*, which I have written as an offering to God for delivering me from sin and giving me the grace and mercy to live holy. I know he will do the same to you, because sin is a destroyer and you don't have to mess with it.

CHAPTER 1: WHAT IS SIN?

I will start by asking these questions and giving answers to them.

What is sin? How did it originate? What are the consequences? And what is the solution?

The first question is, what is sin? And the answer is that sin is a transgression of the laws of the Almighty God. We know that the Almighty God is love, he is holiness, and he is justice. He is mercy, and he is compassion. In fact, his good virtues are indescribable.

Where and how can we find his laws? Well, I strongly believe that you can find his laws in a book called the Bible, which I define as "God in printed matter." No wonder the Bible declares in 2 Timothy 3:16 that "All scriptures is given by inspiration of God, and is profitable for doctrine, for reproof, for correction, for instruction in righteousness: that the man of God may be perfect, thoroughly furnished unto all good works."

The first laws of God was given to Moses, God's servant, but before then, man lived under conscience, for our conscience is the window of the spirit God Almighty has given to man. Mark this distinction very, very carefully: not to animals or any other creatures. The laws that God Almighty gave are found in the Bible. In Exodus 20:1–23, it reads,

> And God spake all these words, saying, I am the Lord thy God, which have brought thee out of the land of Egypt, out of the house of bondage.
>
> Thou shalt have no other gods before me.
>
> Thou shalt not make unto thee any graven image, or any likeness of anything that is in heaven above, or that is in the earth beneath, or that is in the water under the earth; thou shalt not bow down thyself to them, nor serve them: for I the Lord thy God am a jealous God, visiting the iniquity of the fathers upon the children onto the third and fourth generation of them that hate me; and showing mercy unto thousands that love me and keep my commandments.

Thou shalt not take the name of the Lord thy God in vain: for the Lord will not hold him guiltless that taketh his name in vain.

Remember the Sabbath day, to keep it holy. Six days shalt thou labour, and do all thy work: but the seventh day is the Sabbath of the Lord thy God: in it you shalt not do any work, thou, nor thy son, nor thy daughter, thy manservant, nor thy maidservant, nor thy cattle, nor thy stranger that is within thy gates: for in six days the Lord the Lord made heaven and earth, the sea, and all that in them, and rested the seventh day: wherefore the Lord blessed the seventh day and hallowed it.

Honor thy father and thy mother: that thy days may be long upon the land which the Lord thy God giveth thee.

Thou shalt not kill.

Thou shalt not commit adultery.

Thou shalt not steal.

Thou shalt not bear false witness against thy neighbour.

Thou shalt not covet thy neighbour's house, thou shalt not covet thy neighbour's wife, nor his manservant, nor his maidservant, nor his ox, nor his ass, nor anything that is thy neighbour's.

The strange thing is that man, in his fallen nature recorded in Genesis 3:1–24, was incapable to keep God's laws because we are carnal, sold unto sin by Lucifer. But God's laws are spiritual; they are spirit and they are life.

So for us to obey these laws, we need a helper, we need a substitute. Something has to be done. So God became his own substitute.

Another striking question is, how did sin originate? Who is the author? The Bible, God's Word, declared that long before man was created, there was war in heaven. Revelation 12:7–17, a snapshot of it, reads,

And there was war in heaven: Michael and his angels fought against the dragon; and the dragon fought and his angels, and prevailed not; neither was their place found any more in heaven. And the great dragon was cast out, that old serpent, called the Devil, and Satan, which deceiveth the whole world: he was cast out into the earth and his angels were cast out with him. And I heard a loud voice saying in heaven, Now is come salvation and strength, and the kingdom of our God, and the power of his Christ: for the accuser of our brethren is cast down, which accuse them before our God day and night. And they overcame him by the blood of the Lamb, and by the word of their testimony; and they loved not their lives onto death. Therefore rejoice, ye heavens, and ye that dwell in them. Woe to the inhabiters of the earth and of the sea, for the devil is come down unto you, having great wrath, because he knoweth that he hath but a short time.

And when the dragon saw that he was cast unto the earth, he persecuted the woman which brought forth the man child.

The book of Ezekiel 28:14–19 gives another clear explanation of the author of sin, it reads,

Thou art the anointed cherub that covereth; and I have set thee so:

thou was upon the holy mountain of God;

Thou hast walked up and down in the midst of the stones of fire.

Thou was perfect in thy ways from the day that thou wast created, till iniquity was found in thee.

By the multitude of thy merchandise

they have filled the midst of thee with violence, and thou hast sinned:

therefore I will cast thee as profane out of the mountain of God:

and I will destroy thee, O covering cherub,

from the midst of the stones of fire.

Thine heart was lifted up because of thy beauty,

thou has corrupted thy wisdom by reason of thy brightness:

I will cast thee to the ground,

I will lay thee before Kings, that they may behold thee.

Thou hast defiled thy sanctuaries by the multitude of thy iniquities,

by the iniquity of thy traffick;

therefore will I bring forth a fire from the midst of thee,

it shall devour thee,

and I will bring thee to ashes upon the earth

in the sight of all them that behold thee.

All they that know thee among the people shall be astonished at thee:

thou shall be a terror, and never shall thou be any more.

The Bible, God's Word, just gave a full description of who the author of sin is, he was created as one of the archangels that covers the Shechinah, glory and majesty of God Almighty, until the sin of pride was found in him for he declared, "I will descend to the lower heavens and establish my throne and become like the Most High God." That was when God Almighty decided to cast him out of heaven. He and his demons will never smell heaven again. Remember, in the book of Revelation, the Word of God called him "that old serpent that deceiveth the whole world." Before man was created here on planet Earth, Satan was already here, and the account of how he deceived our first parents through Eve, Adam's wife, is recorded in Genesis 3:1–23. The story has it that we fell to Satan's deceit and sin entered into the world. And with that came death, sickness and disease, and all types of catastrophy, and the world became a fallen world. And man was injected with sin genetically until a substitute was given. So positionally, we are completely delivered from the power of sin, but sin will be eradicated in the new heaven and the new earth where dwelleth the righteousness of God. Satan, Lucifer, or dragon is still using the tactics of deceit and lies. He has not changed his formula—he only utilizes different formats. God Almighty been holy and holiness himself, which means it is impossible for God to sin. God is so holy that if he makes a single mistake of sin, he will fail to exist, and everything created, seen and unseen, will disappear and fail to exist anymore. He decided to drive man out of the Garden of Eden because he hates sin so much, he cannot accommodate it. He decided to look for a substitute. No creature was qualified, so he became his own substitute. That substitute is the whole embodiment of the love of God.

CHAPTER 2: TYPES OF SIN

ABOMINATION

Abominations can be done by any man or beast, and they are usually actions that are detestable. The most recent abhorring acts have been the cases of Catholic priests molesting little boys and still calling themselves priests of the Most High God. What a hypocrisy, insulting and blaspheming the Most High God. They practice homosexuality and engage in sexual practices with nuns.

In the olden days, in the city of Benin in Nigeria, if their *oba* dies, they bury him with sixteen human heads. What a travesty and wickedness that is. In the Old Testament in the Word of God, the Bible, during a great famine in Israel, parents ate their children for food. The Hiroshima 1945 atomic bombing and the gassing of six million Jews by Hitler are all cases of abomination. Over and over again, since man fell, from Adam and Eve, our first parents. God been a just and holy god and will judge abomination. There are even cases where women have sex with animals, notably dogs and horses. No wonder God says in his Word, the Bible, Genesis 6:5–6, "And God saw that the wickedness of man was great in the earth, and that every imagination of the thoughts of his heart was only evil continually. And it repented the Lord that he had made man on the earth, and it grieved him at his heart."

ABORTION

Abortion is an abomination against the Almighty God and humanity. Whether the pregnancy is planned or unplanned, to eliminate that child in your womb is horrible. That child you killed as a woman, you don't know whether he or she could have been the next president of any nation, a prophet, or a prominent figure in our world. If God does not want that child, he could not have formed him or her in your womb. If you are involved in abortion, all over the world, you can repent and do it no more. God's Word said in Isaiah 53:1–4, "He was wounded for our transgressions, he was bruised for our iniquities, the chastisement of our peace was placed on him and with his stripes we were healed." You can be forgiven because of the atoning work of Christ at Calvary's cross. Amen.

LYING

God's Word, the Bible, says that a liar cannot stand in God's presence. God hates lying. And a liar is a wicked person, period. Most Bible students know of a case in Acts 5 where a couple sold their property, promising to bring all. But instead, they only brought some of it and lied to the Holy Spirit of God in the presence of Apostle Peter, and both of them instantly died within a short space of time. What of baseball legend Grasshopper who lied to a federal grand jury that he never injected enhancement drugs, but he did? His money and fame could not exonerate him. He was eventually sentenced to two years probation and thirty days of house arrest. He will also do 250 hours of community work and pay a $4,000 fine. What a shame! How are the mighty fallen because of lies.

ADULTERY

Adultery is having sex with another woman who is not your wife when you are married. These are some important and influential men that did it, and it brought great misery not only to themselves and their family but also to God Almighty.

Mr. Quaker Oats got HIV, lost his dignity and respect, and resigned from the NBA (National Basketball Association).

Mr. Artist lost his dignity and respect from his beautiful wife after his rape case.

Former President Utopia was insulted, embarrassed, and impeached by the House of Representatives. He could have lost his presidency if the Senate did not exonerate him. And he went down in history as the only American president who has ever been impeached by the House of Representatives, because of sex. What a shame.

Former North Carolina senator Mr. Bioche lost his presidential ambition, lost his wife to cancer, and lost his respect and dignity because he fathered a child with a woman who is not his wife.

Former governor Inspiration did the same thing, and his wife filed a divorce against him and he completely lost his prestige and dignity.

International Monetary Fund boss Mr. Horse raped an African woman from Guinea who came to answer him at his hotel room in the city of New York and lost his great position, lost his French presidential opportunity, lost his respect and dignity.

Mr. Octopus Sr. fathered a child outside wedlock even though he had a wife who has been on his side for almost fifty years. He lost his spokesmanship as a respected civil rights activist to Rev. Goose and lost his respect and dignity. Bet you, Mr. Thunder Jr., his mentor, could not have done that because he strongly believed that Jesus Christ of Nazareth is Lord and he died for his sins and the sins of the whole world.

Mr. Biochem, a renowned televangelist, left his wife and had sex with his secretary. He lost his ministry PTL (Praise the Lord Ministry) went to prison for six years because of tax malpractices and lost his wife and children through divorce. His wife finally died of cancer recently. What a shame and tragedy. Even though he finally remarried and returned back to grace, his loss has been great. His peace could have been like a river if he did not do that.

What of Mr. Biochemistry, the firebrand renowned televangelist? He had consistent sexual encounters with prostitutes, and he lost his mega ministry, lost his respect and dignity, but he returned back to grace like the prodigal son.

All these could have been prevented if they behaved like Joseph of the Bible, God's Word. When Potiphar's wife wanted to have sex with him by force, he ran away and proclaimed, "I cannot do such a great wickedness against God, against my master, and against myself." People who are born again hate it, having sex outside marriage. I do hate it myself.

GLUTTONY

Gluttony is a sin. Gluttony has many aspects, but I am now referring specifically to food. Food gluttons eat when they are not hungry. They eat to live instead of eating to survive. No wonder the Word of God, the Bible, says that such people make their belly God and mind earthly things. Don't be surprised, gluttons cannot go to heaven. God hates gluttony.

THE TRUE GOD / THE FALSE GOD

Before I go into this topic, I would say that any person who does not worship the God of Abraham, Isaac, and Jacob—the God that is a spirit that our Lord Jesus Christ referred to—is serving a false god and Satan, who wanted worship from the beginning and still wants it today as he camouflages himself with all these. With the spirit of the devil behind false gods or idolatry, some people worship themselves, Satan, money, other human beings, material things, stones, cameras, cars, animals, the sun, the moon, stars, insects, good angels, and fallen angels. Worshipping anything other than God, the Spirit that speaks in tongues (heavenly language), and Jesus Christ (his son, God Incarnate) is worshipping a false god. And God wants us to worship him, the true God, alone. John 4:24 says "God is a Spirit: and they that worship him must worship him in spirit and in truth." Exodus 20:1–6 says,

> And God spake all these words, "I am the Lord thy God, which have brought thee out of the land of Egypt, out of the house of bondage.
>
> Thou shalt have no other gods before me.
>
> Thou shalt not make unto thee any graven image, or any likeness of anything that is in heaven above, or that in the Earth beneath, or that is in the water under the earth: thou shalt not bow thou thyself unto them, nor serve them: for I the Lord thy God, I am a jealous God, visiting the iniquity of the father upon the children Unto the third and fourth generation of them that hate me; and showing mercy, unto thousands that love me, And keep my commandments."

In conclusion, worship belongs only to the true God. If I want to go to heaven when I die, I must worship only him. And if you want to go to heaven when you die, you must do the same. I have eternally chosen to worship only him.

PRIDE

Pride is one of the worst sins that God hates. Lucifer, the devil, is the architect of sin and pride. First Peter 5:5–7 says, "Likewise, ye younger, submit yourselves unto the elder. Yea all of you be subject to one to another, and be clothed with humility: for God resisteth the proud, and giveth grace to the humble. Humble yourselves therefore under the mighty hand of God, that he may exalt you in due time: casting all your care upon him for careth for you." Humility is God's standard and nature. He cannot tolerate pride, and he cannot use someone filled with pride.

Ezekiel 28:17–19 says

Thine heart was lifted up because of thy beauty,

thou hast corrupted thy wisdom by reason of thy brightness:

I will cast thee to the ground,

I will lay thee before kings, that they may behold thee.

Thou hast defiled thy sanctuaries by the multitude of thine iniquities,

by the iniquity of thy traffic;

therefore will I bring forth a fire from the midst of thee,

it shall devour thee

and I shall bring thee to ashes upon the earth

in the sight of all them that behold thee;

thou shall be a terror, and never shalt thou be anymore.

This is a good parallel.

The first message was for the devil, and this one is for Jesus Christ of Nazareth, Almighty God Incarnate, Philippians 2:4–11: "Look not every man on his own things, but every man also on the things of others. Let this mind be in you, which was also in Christ Jesus: who, being in the form of God, thought it not robbery to be equal to God: but made himself of no reputation, and took upon him the form of a servant, and was made in the likeness of men: and being found in fashion as a man, he humbled himself, and became obedient unto death, even the death of the cross. Wherefore God also hath highly exalted him and given him a name which is above every name: that at the name of Jesus of Nazareth, every knee should bow, of things in heaven, and things in earth, and things under the earth and that every tongue should confess that Jesus Christ is Lord, to the glory of God the Father."

HATRED

Hatred, in simple terms, is the act of disliking something or someone. Hatred is the birthright of the devil. In fact, he created and invented it. The idiot bastard, vagabond, nincompoop, fool, garbage, decayed corpse, feces, hated the Almighty God from the beginning. That is why he staged a war with his fallen angels against Jehovah-shammah! And anyone who hates the Almighty is an idiot, bastard, vagabond, nincompoop, garbage, decayed corpse, feces, etc., and can never see the light of life, because Jesus Christ of Nazareth is the Light of the world. Anyone who comes to him shall not walk in the darkness of this world but shall have the light of life. Hatred always leads to murder, Genesis 4:3–18, the first hatred on earth, in the offspring of the first man and woman, Adam and Eve. Their offspring were Cain and Abel. Cain killed his brother Abel because of envy and jealousy because his sacrifice was not acceptable to God but that of his brother was.

The Word of God in Ezekiel 28:19 states, "All they that know thee among the people shall be astonished at thee: thou shall be a terror, and never shalt thou be anymore."

From here we can infer that the casting down of Lucifer or the devil to the earth was when hatred, envy, jealousy, fornication, adultery, masturbation, pornography, homosexuality, lying, seduction, abomination, witchcraft, stealing, and many more followed as its consequence. Then came sickness, death, disease, disappointment, poverty, and war. As a result, the Almighty judged him in the cross of Calvary and created hellfire for him and his angels and those who do not obey the Gospel of our Lord and Savior, Jesus Christ of Nazareth, the God-Man, Savior, Deliverer, Sanctifier, Baptizer with the Holy Spirit, and the Lamb of God slain from the foundations of the world.

Since the devil or Lucifer is the author of hatred, he hates God and everything that obeys God or that are in conformity with the Almighty God. So the devil hates me and every creature that is in heaven and earth. Love is secondary to the devil. He does not know or have love. He does not even love himself nor the angels that follow him. He is really an idiot. God commands us to only hate the devil, his angels, and sin. That is the only thing we are supposed to hate. And to love God the Son, God the Father, God the Holy Spirit, with the whole of our heart, soul, mind, and strength, and to love others as we love ourselves. The human enemies we have are influenced by Lucifer himself when he dominates their hearts.

Over the ages, from Adam and Eve through the progress of civilization, men have shown hatred to each other and the environment they are in.

Let's take slavery for example. Black people where taken as slaves from Africa against their will because the greedy chiefs in Africa were bought by money and gifts, and they sold their own.

The Europeans and United States bought them and used them for selfish means. Today hatred has grown among these groups. But things will get better is my prayer.

The Tower of Babel was allowed by God Almighty. There was confusion of tongues or languages, and God scattered the human family abroad with different languages because they wanted to compete with God (Genesis 11:1–9). With the scattering and language difference increased hatred. Racism became prevalent. Tribalism, injustice, and color became distinguishing factors among humans, which is class distinction. White race flock together, Asians, Indians, and Blacks. And they treat difference with disdain and hatred, except those touched by the love of God, which is in Christ Jesus of Nazareth, our Lord. Don't forget. Let's always go back to the source where we began. The devil, or Lucifer, is the author or originator of hatred, and it infected man when man gave up his birthright to Lucifer in the Garden of Eden. There is hatred between man and animals, insects, and many more other creatures that were friendly to man until Lucifer came into the picture as he is the author of sin.

ENVY

The most typifying form of envy was the Bible account of the offspring of Adam and Eve in Genesis 4:3–18. The Word of God states that Abel was a keeper of the sheep, and Cain, his older brother, was a tiller of the ground. In verse 3, the Word of God declares that "in the process of time, it came to pass that Cain brought of the fruit of the ground an offering unto the Lord. And Abel, his brother, he also brought of the firstlings of his flock and of the fat thereof. And the Lord had respect unto Abel and his offering: but unto Cain and his offering he had no respect. And Cain was wroth, and his countenance fell," and envy set in because God respected his younger brother's sacrifice, which led to him killing his brother. Envy leads to murder, and one feeds the other.

Another typifying story in the Word of God is about the twelve sons of the patriarch Jacob. Joseph and Benjamin were favored more than the other ten because they where borne by the woman Jacob loved, Rachel, and the rest were borne by Leah. And in the process of time, Joseph had a dream where all his siblings, including Jacob, bowed down for him. And his siblings hated him and were envious, because their father had special love for him and made a coat of many colors (Genesis37:1–36). And his siblings sold him to the Ishmaelites, and they took him to the land of Egypt. There God fulfilled the dream.

Envy can be expressed in many forms from family, country, individuals, etc. Always remember, it is one of the manifestations of sin that produces death, and we have to hate sin and eschew it so as to live eternally with God Almighty in heaven. Nothing that defileth shall enter that city.

Another example is about God the Son, Jesus Christ of Nazareth, and how the Pharisees and the Sadducees hated him and were envious of the miracles that he performed among humans (Matthew 15:1–25, 16:1–12).

And they planned for his crucifixion by using Judas as an instrument, but they were doing God a favor that I and you might have eternal life. For Christ Jesus of Nazareth made a public show of all principalities and powers, triumphing over them in it—that is, the cross of Calvary. Amen!

In Colossians 2:13–15, the Word said he spoiled it—that is, principalities and powers. Hallelujah!

JEALOUSY

Let us take a typical natural example of two college students who are taking organic chemistry to end up becoming biochemists or medical doctors. These are two friends. And friend A gets excellent grades in that course, and friend B is not doing well. Friend B becomes jealous of friend A and poisons his food when he comes to visit his house, and A becomes sick and dies.

Here we know that God will eventually judge friend B because he is a righteous judge, but the damage has already been done and was caused by jealousy. Remember these sins feed each other just like in the case of envy. There are many examples of jealousy, but it always leads to death. And God demands that we hate and forsake sin, one of which is jealousy, because he has judged it in the cross of Calvary so that we shall inherit that land whose streets are paved with gold, and in it there is no night for the Lamb and the Father lighteneth the city, and there will be no more death nor crying nor pain nor any other suffering, for the former things are passed away.

MASTURBATION

It simply means having sex with yourself. Only a lunatic and a fool have sex with themselves. The Word of God, the Bible, states in 1 Corinthians 6:18–20, "Flee fornication. Every sin that a man doeth is without the body; but he that committeth fornication sinneth against His own body. What? Know ye not that your body is the temple of the Holy Ghost which is in you, which ye have of God, and ye are not your own. For ye are bought with a price: therefore glorify God in your body, and your Spirit, which are God's." Masturbation is the same as having sex with a woman that is not your wife, and God will judge. Hebrews 13:4 "Marriage is honourable in all, and the bed undefiled: but whoremongers and adulterers God will judge." And God's judgment is disastrous, because he is a God of justice and love at the same time.

PORNOGRAPHY

Only a shameless fool exposes themselves naked in the age where we cover ourselves with clothing, and people that involve themselves in pornography lack wisdom and enhance the spread of diseases. People involved in pornography will be judged by God. God's Word, the Bible, said in Matthew 5:27–28, "Jesus of Nazareth specifically said ye have heard that it was said by them of old time, thou shall not commit adultery: but I say unto you, that whosoever looketh on a woman to lust after her hath committed adultery with her already in her heart." Hence when you look at a naked woman, man, boy, or a girl to lust after them, you have already committed adultery with them in your heart. God will judge.

SEDUCTION

The act of luring is a very dangerous spirit that leads its victims and perpetrators to ultimate destruction. For example, women go half-dressed to lure men into sexual sin and vice versa. Prostitutes are mostly perpetrators of this kind of behavior. God will judge. God's Word said in Mark 9:42, "And whosoever shall offend one of these little ones that believe in me, it is better for him that a millstone were hanged about his neck, and he were cast in to the sea." God will judge seducers.

WITCHCRAFT/SORCERY

This is using demonic powers to harm and to kill the Word of God. The Bible said in John 10:10, "The thief [the devil] cometh but to steal, kill and destroy." Olumba Olumba of Calabar is one of them, but thanks be to God that he is now blind. A blind god—what a shame! He cannot even make himself see. I laugh at a fool like him. The Word of God, the Bible, says in Exodus 22:18, "Thou shall not suffer a witch to live"—you shall kill anyone who is a witch. We have many of them scattered all over the world: palm readers, astrologers, voodoo doctors, and people who use weegie boards are all in the same category, a society of black cats. God said you do not suffer them to live.

STEALING

Is simply taking something that does not belong to you, and thieves are 99 percent of the time murderers. The Word of God said in John 10:10, the devil, the thief, "cometh but to steal, kill and destroy." A murderer is typical of a thief, and he or she is very wicked. Examples are former Nigerian dictators like Sani Abacha, Ibrahim Babangida, and Murdock the criminal financier. And any human that takes and robs people of things that do not belong to them are thieves, and God will judge furiously.

CHAPTER 3:
CONSEQUENCES OF SIN

DEATH

Death affects both children and adults alike. Go to any hospital in the world, and you will see all types of sick humans. Some are dead already, some ready to die, and some are recovered. And from the northern part of the world to the south, east, and west, there are humans that don't even have money to go to hospitals. They die in their homes, and some in the streets. Animals, birds, plants, and all living creatures in the land and sea get sick and die because of sin. Actually, in clear terms, sin turned our world into a fallen world instead of a perfect world. Let us deal with each of the consequences of sin elaborately. Every family on earth has tasted of death, either through sickness, violence, accident, war, or natural cause.

I will give you few examples of death in my family that I can recall. We are now six of us living, thanks be to God. We are supposed to be seven, but my immediate sister died at ten months old. My own father died at seventy-two. My uncles and aunts on my father's and mother's sides, most of them are dead. Most of my cousins are dead. And death comes with sorrow, pain, and grief for those affected. The Word of God, the Bible, said in 1 Corinthians 15 that death is an enemy but it will be swallowed in victory one day. Hallelujah to the Lamb of God! You, my reader, may or may have not bitten an apple out of the experience of death, but you exactly know what I am talking about. Years ago—to be precise, it was four years ago—there was an eight-year-old girl who was playing in the swimming pool of her parents. Without the supervision of an adult, she fell in and drowned. What struck me so much about this incident was that I went to the funeral, and I saw the lifeless body of this little girl lying in state for final view before the burial. I was so much moved with emotion that the memory cannot leave me until I check out here myself. So death strikes infants, children, young men, young women, old men, old women, including other creatures that are living. Plants, animals, arthropods, birds, insects, bacteria, and viruses. Does

Death not have any distinction, class, creed, or race? The answer is no. We all know of Michael Jackson, the king of pop music, known all over the world by both kings and peasants. But death took him in one second, and he died. What of Senator Edward Kennedy, the political giant from the well-renowned Kennedy family. Time will fail me to list well-known men and women who have become victims of death. Creeds cannot prevent death either. Christian, Muslim, Buddhist, Confucian, Pagan, etc., all go through the way of death. The difference with the Christian is that Christians have a hope in a living Savior, a living Fact that cannot be disputed because of the bodily resurrection of Jesus Christ of Nazareth, Almighty God Incarnate. What of race? Can it prevent death? Michael Jackson was of the black race, Senator Edward Kennedy was of a Caucasian origin, and Mahatma Gandhi was brown, but death overpowered them. Class cannot stop death either. Whether you are poor, rich, educated, uneducated, able, or disabled, death overpowers all. That is why the Word of God said in Hebrews 9:27, it is appointed unto men once to die, but after that, the judgment. The most crucial thing is not whether we shall die; that is a given. The important thing is where the person's spirit shall spend eternity. Remember, these things will come to pass. Heaven and earth will pass away, but not an iota or a dot out of God's prophetic Word will fail to be accomplished.

POVERTY

Another great consequence of sin is poverty. Poverty is just the lack of necessary things to enhance life while you are still living. After God created man in the Garden of Eden (Genesis 1; 26–31), God blessed man and told him be fruitful and multiply and replenish the earth and gave him dominion over all living things. When man sinned, the blessing was reversed, and man has to suffer by the sweat of his brow to eat. There are many factors that bring poverty. Some of them are human greed, oppression, suppression, wars, famine, and laziness. There is actually no reason for poverty because God has made enough for everybody, but sin rewrote history.

There are examples of poverty here from where I am writing in San Francisco, California, United States. Humans sleep in the cold winter streets here and the rest of the United States, in a country filled with wealth. I have slept many, many, months in the streets, when I was practicing sin until God changed my cause by the power of the Holy Ghost through his glorious Son, Jesus Christ of Nazareth. Drought in financially less-privileged countries causes a lot of poverty and death. Wars, which I will develop later, is the precursor to refugee Camps, dislocation, separation, poverty, and death. I saw a woman in Nigeria. She had a breast cancer that was bleeding profusely and was begging money with her little boy. At that point, I had no money myself to take her to hospital, but I gave her everything I had that was money, but I kept praying for her. By the grace of God, she will be healed either supernaturally or a good Samaritan who has money will take her to hospital for medical help. Either way, God will heal her, and God will take the glory. The reason why she was in such a deplorable state and was not able to go to hospital is because of poverty. It is a shame to say that in Nigeria, one of the richest oil-producing countries in the world, that is the norm. I took a trip to San Francisco, one of the most glamorous cities in United States and probably the whole world. On a cold winter morning, on Seventh Street on Market, I saw men, women, children, and infants lying down on a hard, cold floor, and around them are skyscrapers, condominiums, and different types of buildings. The reason why they cannot afford to live in those types of structures is because of poverty, which is a precursor of sin. I turned on my television one day, and I saw the ugly sight of a one-year-old child in Mozambique in Africa, literally skeleton and bones because of malnutrition. Her parents don't even have money to buy milk for her. I know of cases in Nigeria, Brazil, Mexico, India, etc., where children ages between two to sixteen years old are sent out to the streets to beg for money by their parents, and they become victims of violence, disease, prostitution, drugs, and untimely deaths at the hands of rival gangs and brutal police.

Poverty is a precursor of sin. When God created us in the Garden of Eden, everything was there for us. We had shelter. We had food and sound health. Everything was there in abundance. But sin derailed it, and we became victims of our own circumstances. Hallelujah! But God promised us a new heaven and a new earth where dwelleth the righteousness of God. The lost paradise will be fully regained. Apostle Paul, writing by the inspiration of the Holy Spirit, wrote that the first Adam was a living soul, but the Second Adam was a quickening Spirit. He was clearly referring to King Jesus, that great Spirit that lives in us. King Jesus, speaking to his disciples, once told them that they will always have the poor with them. He was referring to this present earthly existence. In eternity, it will not be so. In the Gospel of John, chapter 14:1–3, King Jesus of Nazareth, said, "Let not your heart be troubled: you believe in me and you believe in my father, for in my father's house are many mansions; if it were not so I would have told you. I go to prepare a place for you, and if I go and prepare a place for you, I will come again and take you, so that where I am, you will be there also."

I would like to expose what Lucifer hides from us while we are still alive, and that is the fact that poverty ends here on planet Earth. When we wear a new body, we do not need food or shelter or want, for the Lord God Almighty will be that temple, and we shall glory in him, forever and forever.

SICKNESS AND DISEASE

Sickness came as a result of sin. And the dictionary explanation of sickness is "the impairment of normal physiological function affecting part or all of an organism." Disease is "an impairment of health, or a condition of abnormal functioning," and is also as a result of sin. Here are some of the diseases known to man. HIV, glaucoma, genital herpes, syphilis, gonorrhea, chlamydia, cancer, trichomoniasis, sickle cell anemia, blindness, diabetes, high blood pressure, tuberculosis, schizophrenia, lunacy, Ebola, leprosy, asthma, heart attack, stroke, brain hemorrhage, and many more. The Word of God states that with the stripes of Jesus Christ of Nazareth we are healed, past, present, future. His thirty-nine stripes takes care of nearly thirty-nine types of diseases known to man. Each stripe obliterates each disease if you apply your faith to the finished work of Christ at Calvary's cross. For he did not die in vain. He died to obliterate our sins and disease so that I and you will have the gift of eternal life. It is a terrible, unimaginable thing for any spirit to spend eternity with Lucifer and his demons in hellfire prepared for them, not for us.

WAR

One of the great consequences of sin is war. War has claimed more human lives in history than all sickness and disease put together, including all accidents and other calamities put together. War is horrible, so to say. Some of the examples of war that we know are as follows: the First and Second World Wars, the Nigerian civil war, the Liberian war, the war between Israel and the Palestinians, the Rwandan war, the Libyan war, the Iraq and Afghanistan wars, the war between Cain and Abel, and family wars. I will discuss each of these then one by one. Remember, war started in heaven, orchestrated by Lucifer, God's enemy and my enemy and your enemy. The First and Second World Wars were hopeless and devastating. I pray the world will never see another war. I quote from one of my sources, which you can download at http://www.harrymcfee.com/history.html. It reads, "Britain's bomber command while our fighters squadrons were often our own. Some fighter pilots had volunteered as part of the Royal for the battle of Britain and took their training in Britain. Others of the BCATP were trained here in Canada and then sent overseas making a significant contribution to the wars effort. Then German V2 rockets delivered their payload on London, as did the dreaded doodlebug bombs. Jet engine airplanes were developed in both England and Germany. When peace in Europe was finally declared, on 6th May 1945, many pilots and aircrew returned home. The war with Japan then continued in the Pacific until the dropping of the atomic bomb on Hiroshima and Nagasaki in August and final surrender of Japan occurred September, 1945."

As I said before at the beginning of this book, war started in heaven. Lucifer, or Satan, waged war against the Almighty God and his Christ but could not prevail because he and his angels were driven out by the power of God. And since then, humans and all creatures are at war with each other. And that takes us to the first war recorded among humans: the war between two brothers, Cain and Abel. It is recorded in the Word of God in Genesis 4:1–26, how Cain slew his brother Abel because of jealousy for God accepted Abel's burnt offering and rejected his.

Another episode is my schoolmate Cyprain Odumodu. We went to school at Dennis Memorial Grammar School, Onitsha. His younger brother axed him to death over a dispute on family real estate when he returned from United States to manage this family estate because his father was a very wealthy man. Another war, which will conclude the history of the present earth, is the war of Armageddon recorded in God's Word, Revelation 19:11–21 and 20:1–3, and Satan will be bound and thrown into the bottomless pit for a thousand years before he and his angels and they who disobey the Gospel of our Lord Jesus Christ are cast in the lake of fire forever.

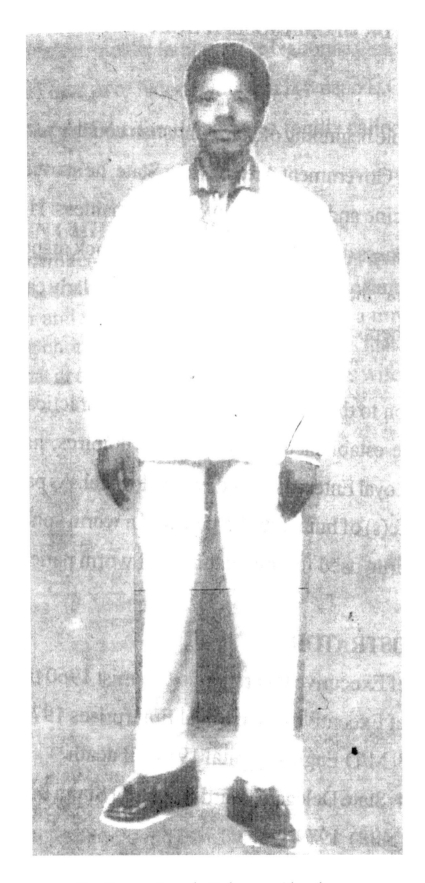

Dr. Ijeoma Joseph Ogbonna Okerekeugo

My father's straight portrait in his younger days

My father and mother at church

My inlaw Robinson Mba and my Aunt Mercy Mba and their children

My water baptism at Assemblies of God church fegge Onitsha Nigeria

Me and Jeff Bosakawski;
kidding around at the house of prayer. I pray we meet in heaven.

Me and my two sister's Adanma and Onyinyechukwu

My father and mother and my brother Nnanyelugo Okerekeugo

My Aunt that took care of me as an infant to my adult years long
life and good health to her. I love you Dadam Adeline.

Dr. Francis Udeh;

the pastor that wedded me and my wife

Me and my wife during our traditional marriage

My pastor Flavio Carvalho and his family

Dr. I.O Okerekeugo
with his Wife & Children in family retreat

Papa and Mama's Wedding Ceremony in 1959

FIRST AND SECOND WORLD WARS

The First and Second World Wars have been fought. My dear mother, Mrs. Helen Ngozi Okerekeugo, was born at the beginning of the Second World War in 1939, bless her beautiful heart. And my father, the late Dr. Joseph Ijeoma Okerekeugo, was born toward the tail end of the First World War, bless his beautiful heart.

Let me take a brief excerpt from http://www.harrymcfee.com/history.html. Of course, millions of human beings perished in these wars. It reads, "The war in Japan then continued in the Pacific, until the dropping of the atomic bomb on Hiroshima and Nagasaki in August and final surrender of Japan occurred September, 1945. There were 55,000 airmen whose graves are unknown as their remains were never found. Their names appear on the memorial at Runnymede, England. In addition to the jet engine being introduced during wartime, the atomic bomb brought us into a power struggle with Russia, aptly named the 'cold war' which was a test of nerves. Neither Russia nor the USA wanted to start a war, but neither would lay down their arms until the 1990s. Other less intense but still very serious wars of Korea and Vietnam and presently the Afghanistan! Iraq wars would always remind us of worldwide wars. Of course we all hope that there will be peace in our time."

The Biafran-Nigerian civil war, was the worst thing I experienced as a boy growing up. It started in 1966, when I was only six years old. I walked nine miles with my brother Ndubuizu Ihechukwu Okerekeugo, who was only three years old, accompanied with our mother, who was a very young woman then. Sometimes in a child's eye, I saw bones of dead bodies even though I was shielded by my parents, Dr. Ijeoma and Mrs. Helen Ngozi Okerekeugo. I saw children of my age and younger looking like skeletons because of starvation. In a nutshell, it was nightmare for a child of that age.

Here is just one of the excerpts on the Nigerian civil war from http://en.wikipedia.org/wiki/Nigerian_Civil_War. It reads

> To expel the Biafrans from the mid-west, as well as defend the west side and attack Biafra from the west as well. As Nigerian forces retook the mid-west, the Biafran military administrator declared the Republic of Benin on 19 September 1967.

Although Benin City was retaken by the Nigerians on 22 September, the Biafrans succeeded in their primary objective by tying down as many Nigerian Federal troops as much as they could. Gen. Gowon also launched an offensive into Biafra south from the Niger Delta to the riverine area using the bulk of the Lagos garrison command under Colonel Benjamin Adekunle (called the Black Scorpion) to form the 3rd Infantry Division, which was later named the 3rd Marine Commando. As the war continued, the Nigerian army recruited amongst a wider area, including Yoruba, Itshekiri, Urhobo, Edo, Ijaw, and etc. Four battalions of the Nigerian 2nd Infantry Division were needed to drive the Biafrans back and eliminate their territorial gains made during the offensive. The Nigerians were repulsed three times as they attempted to cross the river Niger during October, resulting in the loss of thousands of troops, dozens of tanks and equipment. The first attempt by the 2nd Infantry division on 12 October to cross the Niger from Asaba to the Biafran city of Omtsha cost the Nigerian federal army over 5,000 soldiers killed, wounded, captured, or missing.

From 1968 onward, the war fell into a form of stalemate, with Nigerian forces unable to make significant advances into the remaining areas of Biafran control due to stiff resistance and major defeats in Abagana, Arochukwu, Oguta, Umuahia, Onne, Ikot Ekpene, etc. But another Nigerian offensive from April to June 1968 began to close the ring around the Biafrans with further advances on the two northern fronts and the capture of Port Harcourt on 19 May 1968. The blockade of the surrounded Biafrans led to humanitarian disaster when it emerged that there was widespread civilian hunger and starvation in the besieged Igbo areas. The Biafran government claimed that Nigeria was using .hunger as a weapon. . .

The war in Liberia that lasted fourteen years, produced one million refugees and destroyed two hundred thousand lives. The incidents that caused the war are as follows: In 1980, Samuel Doe, a Liberian army master sergeant, seized power through a bloody coup by assassinating President Tolbert and executing thirteen of his cabinet members. In 1989, Charles Taylor, a military man who was part of Doe's cabinet, entered Liberia through Cote D'Ivoire, seeking to overthrow Samuel Doe's regime. This resulted in a civil war that was brought to an end by African peacekeepers in 1996. In 1996, Charles Taylor was elected as president in an election against Ms. Ellen Johnson Sirleaf. In 1999, a second civil war was started by a rebel group called Liberians United for Reconciliation and Democracy in Northern Liberia. Taylor's action provoked this war, which lasted for seven years. In 2003, a second rebel group surfaced in Southern Liberia further, escalating the conflict. The combined rebel forces shut down the country. In the midst of this chaos, Charles Taylor fled the country to Nigeria. During the summer of set 2003, Nigerian peacekeeping forces under the United Nations and US Marine expeditionary forces secured the country. The governance reform commission was set up on June 2003 as part of the deal to end the civil war. The commission was chaired by Ms. Ellen Johnson Sirleaf until 2005 when she ran for president.

This is the consequence of sin, war. Excerpts are from http://www.mtholyoke.edu/boate2Oc/worldpolitics/Briefhistory.html.

Another case of war was the Rwanda war. In 1994, there was a mass murder of eight hundred thousand in the small East African nation of Rwanda. Over the course of approximately one hundred days (from the assassination of Juvénal Habyarimana and Cyprien Ntaryamira on April 6) through mid-July, over five hundred thousand people were killed, according to the Human Rights Watch estimate. Estimates of the death toll have ranged between five hundred thousand and one million, or as much as 20 percent of the country's total population. It was the culmination of longstanding ethnic competition and tensions between the minority Tutsi, who had controlled power for centuries, and the majority Hutu peoples, who had come to power in the rebellion of 1959–62 and had overthrown the Tutsi monarchy.

All because of the consequences of sin that started in heaven when Lucifer led a rebellion against the Almighty God, because of pride.

The first human-recorded war is found in God's Word, the Bible, Genesis 4:1–17. Cain and Abel were Adam and Eve's children. Abel was a hunter, and Cain was a farmer. In the course of time, they brought their sacrifices to God. Abel brought the best to God, and Cain brought something not acceptable to God. And God accepted Abel's sacrifice and rejected that of Cain. Cain became jealous and killed his brother, and God cursed Cain. All murderers are cursed by God.

The final war, will be the war of Armageddon recorded in Revelation 20:1–15. The war has already been won in the cross of Calvary. It will be finalized. Verses 1–3 read, "And I saw an angel come down from heaven, having the key of the bottomless pit and a great chain in his hand. And he laid hold on the Dragon, that old Serpent which is the Devil, and Satan, and bound him a thousand years, and cast him into the bottomless pit, and shut him up, and set a seal upon him, that he should deceive the nations no more, till the thousand years be fulfilled: and after that he should be loosed for a little season."

Verses 6–15 read,

Blessed and holy is he that hath part in the first resurrection: on such the second death hath no power, but they shall be priests of God and of Christ, and shall reign with him a thousand years.

And when the thousand years are expired, Satan shall be loosed out of his prison and shall go out to deceive the nations which are in the four quarters of the earth, Gog and Magog, to gather them together for battle: the number of whom is as the sand of the sea. And they went up on the breadth of the earth, and compassed the camp of the saints about, and the beloved city: and fire came down from God out of heaven and devoured them. And the devil that deceived them was cast into the lake of fire and brimstone, where the beast and the false prophets are, and shall be tormented day and night forever and ever.

And I saw a great white throne, and him that sat on it, from whose face the earth and the heaven fled away; and there was found no place found for them. And I saw the dead, small and great, stand before God; and the books were opened: and another book was opened, which is the book of life: and the dead were judged out of those things written in the books, according to their works. And the sea gave up the dead which were in it; and death and hell delivered up the dead which were in them: and they were judged every man according to their works. And death and hell were cast into the lake of fire. This is the second death. And whosever not found written in the book of life was cast into the lake of fire.

Thanks to you, Lord Jesus, because the war has already been won, and shame to you, Satan. You have already been defeated.

NATURAL DISASTERS

After man sinned, we started immediately to experience natural disasters, because as the Holy Ghost put it with the mouth of Apostle Paul, "all creation groaneth awaiting the day of redemption when Christ will appear in glory." Earthly creation became hostile to man and animals, plants, and insects. We now have earthquakes, hurricanes, flooding, volcanoes, and many more. Our God has promised a new heaven and a new earth were dwelleth the righteousness of God.

CHAPTER 4:
SOLUTION TO SIN

Solution to sin, whose penalty is death, came when God the Son was crucified in the cross of Calvary at Golgotha. He bled and gave up his Spirit, the Holy Spirit. For the Holy Spirit is the Spirit of Christ. After three days, according to God's determinate counsel, God the Father returned the Spirit to the body prepared from the foundation of the world to bear our sins, and he was raised from the dead. For it was impossible for death to hold him. He has power to lay down his life. He has power to take it up again. Such commandments he received from the Father. As a result, anyone from the north, south, east, west of planet Earth who applies his or her faith to the finished work at the cross of Calvary will automatically have the gift of eternal life when they leave this present life, or earthly existence, and will not be a part of the second death that is hellfire. For the devil and his demons and all those who do not accept the Gospel of our Lord and Savior, Jesus Christ of Nazareth, have already been judged to inherit hellfire.

SCRIPTURE REFERENCES

Colossians 2:14–15

Blotting the handwriting of ordinances that was against us, which was contrary to us, and took it out of the way, nailing it to his cross; and having spoiled principalities and powers, He made a shew of them openly, triumphing over them in it.

1 Corinthians 15:44–47

It is sown a natural body; it is raised a spiritual body.

There is a natural body and there is a spiritual body. And so it is written, The first man Adam was made a living soul; the last Adam was made a quickening spirit. How be it that was not first which is spiritual, but that which is natural; and afterward that which is spiritual. The first man is of the earth, earthy; the second man is the Lord from heaven.

Hebrews 9:22–28

And almost all things are by law purged with blood; and without shedding of blood is no remission.

It was therefore necessary that the patterns in the heavens should be purified with these; but the heavenly things themselves with better sacrifice than these. For Christ is not entered into the holy places made with hands, which are the figures of the true; but into heaven itself, now to appear in the presence of God for us: nor yet that he should offer himself often, as the high priest entereth into the holy place every year with blood of others; for then must he often have suffered since the foundation of the world: but now once in the end of the world hath he appeared to put away sin by the sacrifice of himself. And as it is appointed unto men once to die, but after this the judgement: so Christ was once offered to bear the sins of many; and unto them that look for him shall he appear The second time without sin unto salvation.

CHAPTER 5:
THE BLESSINGS OF GOD

THE POWER OF THE HOLY SPIRIT

The Holy Spirit is the third person of the Trinity. He is the Creator of the whole universe; things seen and unseen, he made them all. He is equal with God the Son and God the Father. They work in unity. When God the Father and God the Son are speaking, God the Holy Spirit is speaking at the same time. He is the Spirit of truth, love, holiness, mercy, and justice. The Word of God explained him briefly in the book of Galatians, chapter 5:22–26: "But the fruit of the Spirit is love, joy, peace, longsuffering, gentleness, goodness, faith, meekness, temperance: against such there is no law. And they that are Christ's have crucified the flesh with the affections and lusts. If we live in the Spirit, let us also walk in the Spirit. Let us not be desirous of vain glory, provoking one another, envying one another."

He is our comforter. God's Word said in John 14:13–21,

And whatsoever ye shall ask in my name, that will I do, that the Father may be glorified in the Son. If ye ask any thing in my name, I will do it.

If you love me, keep my commandments. And I will pray the Father, and he shall give another Comforter, that he may abide with you forever; even the Spirit of truth; whom the world cannot receive, because it seeth him not, neither knoweth him: but ye know him; for be dwelleth with you, and shall be in you. I will not leave you comfortless: I will come to you. Yet a little while, and the world seeth me no more; but you see me: because I live, ye shall live also. And that day ye shall know that I am in my Father, and ye in me, and I in you. He that hath my commandments, and keepeth them, he it is that loveth me: and he that loveth shall be loved of my Father, and I will love him, and will manifest myself to him.

Personally, I have different encounters where I experienced the power of the Holy Spirit. I rented a room from an old man. Things went well initially, but as time progressed, the relationship went sour. This particular morning, he was having a heart problem and was rushed to the nearby hospital. I wanted to visit him in the hospital to show compassion, but the Holy Spirit told me inside, "Do not go." A few minutes later, his in-law called my number and stated that he was saying things so delusional toward me that I should not visit. Who knows what could have happened, but the Holy Ghost had already warned me. What a glorious Spirit! Hallelujah!

In another encounter, my personal car, a 1991 Honda, had a brake leak, but I did not know, and I had travelled many miles to a city in the United States called San Francisco. Initially, I was thinking I should change the brake, but the Holy Ghost told me open the hood. And I did, and behold, the brake oil was totally empty.

In 1995, I was operating a taxi in the city of El Cerrito in the Contra Costa county of the United States, and I picked up this young man from their ban station to a street called Key Boulevard, and he directed me to a dead end. He pulled a short gun and pointed it behind my head and pulled the trigger, but the bullet recoiled because the power of the Holy Spirit stopped it. Weeks later, he returned the wallet to my address. At the time, I was living with a fellow Nigerian called Andy Nwankwo. He is a witness to this returned wallet. What a glorious Spirit! Hallelujah!

In 1989, I was driving a taxi in the city of Oakland, and I picked up four young men from one of their malls called Eastmont Mall, and they directed me to a street called Eighty-First avenue. As we stopped, one of them pointed a machine gun at my back and ordered me to keep walking, but he did not shoot because of the power of the Holy Ghost. As I walked three-quarters of a mile, I heard rounds of gunshots. They were shooting at my car. When the company I was driving for towed the car to their garage the following morning, it was full of bullet holes. Hallelujah! What a glorious Spirit! Amen.

In 2002, right after my father, Dr. Ijeoma Ogbonna Okerekeugo passed away to eternity awaiting the Rapture, I was driving a taxi with Yellow Cab San Francisco, and I fell asleep while the car was in motion, but the power of the Holy Ghost stopped the car in the middle of an intersection in the city of San Francisco, United States, called Duboce Street and Valencia Street. What a glorious Spirit! Glory to the Lamb of God who gave his Spirit.

In 1987, when I barely knew how to drive, I picked up a car with a taxi company called Friendly Cab in the city of Oakland. I entered the freeway, not looking, just two feet from a trailer that could have crushed me, but the power of the Holy Ghost prevented that accident from happening. Hallelujah to the Lamb of God who gave his Spirit.

I was a fornicator for many years, but when the power of the Holy Ghost arrested me, I obtained mercy from God to live holy. What a glorious Spirit, hallelujah! Amen. Now I am married, and the love of God constraineth me from sin (1 Corinthians 5:14), and I made a covenant with God to hate sin and another covenant that I will not have sex with myself or anything or anybody except my wife the remaining days of my life. Thank God for the power of the Holy Ghost.

Now remember, the Holy Spirit hates sin and the devil and his demons. That is why his Baptizer, Jesus Christ of Nazareth, made a public show of all principalities and powers in the cross of Calvary, triumphing over them in it. His main job is to bring glory and honor to Jesus Christ of Nazareth and to convict the world and us of sin and also to comfort those that are born again by the Holy Spirit.

I know that athletes build up their muscles by exercising so that they can be strong so they can compete to win in the events they specialize in. The same applies to spiritual warfare from here to heaven. As a result, Apostle Jude, writing by the power of the Holy Ghost, admonishes us to pray in the Spirit twenty-four hours a day. Jude 1:20–21 state, "But ye beloved, building up yourselves on your most holy faith, praying in the Holy Ghost, keep your selves in the love of God, looking for the mercy of our Lord Jesus Christ unto eternal life." I believe that what Apostle Jude was talking about is that for you to keep yourself in the love of God, you must pray in the Spirit constantly. What is happening is that your Spirit man communicates with God, who is a spirit, and the fruits of the Spirit will be fully manifested in your life, and you will have power over self, which is the flesh, sin, Satan, and his demons. Try it and see. Oh! Beloved children of God that are born-again, and see what happens in your spiritual life. We know that an iron magnet attracts only iron and that birds of the same feather fly together, which means they that are born again by the Spirit of our God.

When Christ appears in the air, the Spirit of Christ, which is the Holy Spirit, will snatch them up as a magnet, and they will meet the Lord in the air. Apostle Paul, writing by the Holy Ghost, explained it this way, in Romans 8:8–11, and it reads,

> So then they that are in the flesh cannot please God.
>
> But you are not in the flesh, but in the Spirit, if so be that the Spirit of God dwell in you. Now if any man have not the Spirit of Christ, he is none of his. And if Christ be in you, the body is dead because of sin; but the Spirit is life because of righteousness. But if the Spirit of him that raised up Jesus from the dead dwell in you, He that raised up Christ from the dead shall also quicken your mortal bodies by his Spirit that dwell in you.

That's it—if his Spirit dwells in you when Christ appears in the air, his Spirit will snatch you up.

He is also the Spirit of truth. Ananias and Sapphira lied to him, and he exposed them. They died physically and spiritually.

He is also the Spirit of holiness, he dealt with me on this issue, and I obtained mercy from him to live holy. He is the Spirit of wisdom, compassion, mercy, and love. He is also the Spirit of justice. Due to his immeasurable love, he grieves when we sin against him if we are born-again. He is also our intercessor as he helps our infirmities. Romans 8:26 says "Likewise the Spirit helpeth our infirmities: for we know not what we should pray for as we ought: but the Spirit itself maketh intercession for us with groanings which cannot be uttered."

He is our teacher and also our comforter. He is the Spirit of peace and tranquility. What a glorious Spirit! Hallelujah! Thank God for the Holy Ghost.

THE BLOOD OF JESUS CHRIST OF NAZARETH

The Word of God states that life is in the blood, which means that blood has a special function—it is where the life of any animal or man is. That is why they give blood transfusion to humans and animals to keep them alive when they have shortage of blood. In the Word of God, the

Bible, if you read through Leviticus, you will see how the blood of birds and animals was used for cleansing sin. The Word of God states that the blood of bulls and goats and humans could not wash away sin, hence Jesus of Nazareth, God's Lamb, shed his blood and washed away our sins (Hebrews 9:14, 9:22, and 9:28). Actually in summary, without the shedding of blood of Jesus Christ of Nazareth, we cannot go to heaven. And there is tremendous power in the precious blood of Jesus Christ of Nazareth, power that is greater than any power. The blood of Jesus Christ of Nazareth supersedes every power. The blood saves, heals, and sanctifies, and destroys and consumes all the power of the devil and his demons. Now you will not misuse the grace of God in vain by committing the same sin over and over again and seeking the blood to cleanse you. Jesus of Nazareth, the only bearer of cleansing blood who takes me and you to eternal life, told the impotent man at the pool of Bethsaida, "Go and sin no more lest a worst thing come upon you."

First John 1:7–10 gives us a full illustration of the power of the blood. Verse 7 gets my attention. It states, "But if we walk in the light, as he is in the light, we have fellowship one with another, and the blood of Jesus Christ his Son cleanseth us from all sin." Here, I strongly believe that if we practice sin or make sin a daily lifestyle, we are not even born again and not even walking in the light. Because they who are born again live holy, but sometimes they sin, and the blood of Jesus Christ of Nazareth cleanses them from all sins.

THE BIBLE

The Bible is God in printed form. Every statement or word or letter written in the Bible is directly from the mouth of God. The Spirit of God, the Holy Spirit, moved on humans and they wrote as God dictated. Amos 3:7 says, "Surely the Lord will do nothing, but he revealeth his secret unto his servants the prophets." Second Timothy 3:16–17 says, "All scripture is given by the inspiration of God, and is profitable for doctrine, for reproof, for correction, for instruction in righteousness: that the man of God may be perfect, thoroughly furnished unto all good works." As a result, every word in the Bible is true because God cannot lie. It is impossible for God to lie (Titus 1:2). As a result, every prophetic utterance in the Bible must be fulfilled. The Bible has sixty-six books written by different authors at different times, and each author was inspired by the Spirit of God, the Spirit that raised up the body of Jesus Christ of Nazareth from the grave. All the authors were Jews, based on the covenant the Almighty

God made with father Abraham, saying "Out of your seed shall all the nations of the earth be blessed." Remember, studying the genealogy of father Abraham, he came from Ur of the Chaldees and migrated to Canaan, the present territory of the Jewish nation. The books include Genesis, Exodus, Leviticus, Numbers, Deuteronomy, Joshua, Judges, Ruth, 1 and 2 Samuel, l and 2 Kings, 1 and 2 Chronicles, Ezra, Nehemiah, Esther, Job, the Psalms, the Proverbs, Ecclesiastes, the Song of Solomon, Isaiah, Jeremiah, Lamentations, Ezekiel, Daniel, Hosea, Joel, Amos, Obadiah, Jonah, Micah, Nahum, Habakkuk, Zephaniah, Haggai, Zechariah, Malachi. And the New Testament, written by the covenant of the blood of Jesus Christ of Nazareth, God's only begotten Son, include Matthew; Mark; Luke; John; the Acts; Romans; 1 and 2 Corinthians; Galatians; Ephesians; Philippians; Colossians; 1 and 2 Thessalonians; 1 and 2 Timothy; Titus; Philemon; Hebrews; James; 1 and 2 Peter; 1, 2, and 3 John; Jude; and Revelation. Read it, whether you are from Africa, Asia, North and South America, Europe, or the Middle East, etc. Read it, believe it, obey it, and you shall have the gift of eternal life, which means your spirit shall live eternally.

THE DEITY OF JESUS CHRIST OF NAZARETH

Before I say anything about the deity of Jesus Christ, let us see what the Word of God, the Bible, says about him. In Gospel of John chapter 1, verses 2–4, 10–16, it reads, "In the beginning was the Word, and the Word was with God, and the Word was God. All things were made by him; and without him was not anything made that was made. In him was life and the life was the light of men."

He was in the world, and the world was made by him, and the world knew him not. He came unto his own and his own received him not, but as many as received him, to them gave he power to become the sons of God, even to them that believe on his name, which were born not of blood, nor of the will of the flesh, nor of the will of man, but of God. And the Word was made flesh, and dwelt among us, and we beheld his glory, the glory as of the only begotten of the Father, full of grace and truth.

John bare witness of him, and cried, saying, This was he of whom I spake, he that cometh after me, is preferred before me: for he was before me. And of his fullness, have all we received, and grace for grace. For the law was given by Moses, but grace and truth came by Jesus Christ. No man hath seen God at any time; the only begotten Son, which is in the bosom of the Father, he hath declared him. (John 1:10–16)

Bosom can be interpreted "beloved; intimate": a bosom friend. Or you can say, "in the chest of the Father." In Philippians chapter 2, verses 5–11, the Word of God states, "Let this mind be in you, which was also in Christ Jesus: who being in the form of God, thought it not robbery to be equal with God, but made himself of no reputation, and took upon him the form of a servant, and made in the likeness of men, and being found in the fashion of a man, he humbled himself, and became obedient unto death, even the death of the cross; wherefore God hath also hath highly exalted him and given him a name which is above every name, that at the name of Jesus every knee shall bow, of things in heaven, and things in earth, and things under the earth and that every tongue should confess that Jesus Christ is Lord, to the glory of God the Father."

There is nothing much I can say than what the Word of God has said. I say that Jesus Christ of Nazareth is the unlimited Spirit that created everything, but he became like us so as to redeem us to himself. What a glorious miracle, hallelujah! To support what I just said, God's Word said in Hebrews chapter 7, verses 26–28, "For such an high priest became us, who is holy, harmless, undefiled, separate from sinners, and made higher than the heavens. Who needed not daily, as those high priests, to offer up sacrifice, first for his own sins, and then for the people's: for this he did once, when he offered up himself. For the law maketh men high priests which have infirmity; but the word of the oath, which was since the law, maketh the Son who is consecrated for evermore."

CHAPTER 6: THE DEVIL

THE DEVIL

Let's take a look at the devil. Who is the devil? a curious mind might ask, and how did the Almighty God allow him tempt man to disobey him? Well, the answer is that the devil was the leader of the angelic host in heaven that leads the angelic choir. Remember, the Almighty God enjoys praise because he is more than worthy to receive all the praise, adoration, majesty, and dominion; because he has created all things for the main purpose of worshipping him (Revelation 12:7–17; Ezekiel 28:14–19).

Again, he can do without anything worshipping him, whether the archangels, cherubim, and seraphim or all the creations we see with our eyes in the heavens and the earth, including us humans. Why? Because he is self-contained. He wants his creations to be in fellowship with him so they can be constantly blessed spiritually, physically, and otherwise. It's just like a pregnant woman carrying a baby. The baby can only be sustained and live from the food he or she gets from his or her mother. Thus all creation needs fellowship with God so that they can be blessed. Hence, Lucifer conducted the angelic choir and was also the angel that covered the glory of God. Wait a minute—can you look at the sun directly for just, say, three minutes? You will automatically be blinded. That is nothing compared to the glory of the Almighty God (Genesis 3:8; Psalm 103:1–22; Psalm 98:1–9; Psalm 100:1–5). Remember, in the book of Revelation, the description of the glorified Christ as Apostle John saw him in the isle of Patmos. The truth of the Word of God declares that his eyes are like the flame of fire, his total appearance is like the sun in its full strength, his feet are like brass, and his voice is like the sound of many waters, and John fell as dead when he saw him. And he picked him up, declaring that he is Alpha and Omega, the beginning and the end, he was dead and now he is alive, the first fruit of those that rose from the dead, and that he has the keys of death and the grave, which he took from Lucifer when he went to the grave and conquered death by taking the keys from him, and our mortal bodies will be quickened when he returns. That was the glory that Lucifer covered in heaven. He could not behold it. He just covered it.

One day, pride entered Lucifer because of his position, and he decided to stage a war against God to overthrow him. As a result there was war in heaven, which means war started in heaven. Well, as usual, his doom was determined to be eternal death. The book of Ezekiel chapter 14 states that Lucifer and the angels who fell with him were created perfect until iniquity and pride was found in him. That pride brought his end, according to Ezekiel from 14 to 20.

THE SYNONYMS OF SATAN

Synonyms are two words that can be interchanged in a context. They are said to be synonymous relative to that context. A synonym is a word or expression that has the same or almost the same meaning. Now since we know what a synonym is, the synonym of Satan in a compound word is sin.

The Word of God gave us all of them in Galatians 5:18–21. We have "But if ye be led by the Spirit, ye are not under the law; now the works of the flesh are manifest, which are these: adultery [synonym of Satan], fornication [synonym of Satan], uncleanness [synonym of Satan], lasciviousness [synonym of Satan], idolatry [synonym of Satan], witchcraft [synonym of Satan], hatred [synonym of Satan], variance [synonym of Satan], emulations [synonym of Satan], wrath [synonym of Satan], strife [synonym of Satan], seditions [synonym of Satan], heresies [synonym of Satan], envyings [synonym of Satan], murders [synonym of Satan], drunkenness [synonym of Satan], revellings [synonym of Satan], and such like; of the which I tell you before, as I have also told you in time past, that they which do such things shalt not inherit the kingdom of God."

In Romans 1:24–31, verses 29–32 list "unrighteousness [synonym of Satan], fornication [synonym of Satan], wickedness [synonym of Satan], covetousness [synonym of Satan], maliciousness [synonym of Satan], envy [synonym of Satan], murder [synonym of Satan], debate [synonym of Satan], deceit [synonym of Satan], malignity [synonym of Satan], whispering [synonym of Satan], backbiting [synonym of Satan], haters of God [synonym of Satan], despiteful [synonym of Satan], pride [synonym of Satan], boasting [synonym of Satan], inventors of evil things [synonym of Satan and his demons], disobedient to parents [synonym of Satan], without understanding [synonym of Satan], covenant breakers [synonym of Satan], without natural affection [synonym of Satan], implacable [synonym of Satan], unmerciful [synonym of Satan], who knowing the judgment of God, that they which commit such things are worthy of death, not only do the same, but have pleasure in them that do them." Lesbianism [synonym of Satan], homosexuality [synonym of Satan], fear [synonym of Satan]. Revelation 21:8 adds, "But the fearful [synonym of Satan], unbelief [synonym of Satan], abomination [synonym of Satan], murder [synonym of Satan], whoremongering [synonym of Satan], sorcery [synonym of Satan], idolatry [synonym of Satan], lies [synonym of Satan]" and humans who participate in these shall have their part in the lake which burneth with fire and brimstone, which is the second death.

Satan fever

Satan amyotrophic lateral sclerosis

Satan obsessive-compulsive disorder

Satan advanced multiple myeloma

Satan cancer

Satan acute leukemia

Satan arthritis (psoriatic)

Satan muscle spasm (tetany)

Satan pulmonary tuberculosis

Satan celiac disease

Satan attention deficit hyperactivity disorder

Satan fatigue urination sickness

Satan influenza

Satan yeast infection

Satan schizophrenia

Satan infectious diseases

Satan flesh-eating bacteria controversy (Morgana's Observatory)

Satan AIDS

Satan adult Still's disease

Satan stroke

Satan leprosy

Satan complex post-traumatic stress disorder

Satan heart attack

Satan asthma

Satan lupus

Satan Huntington's disease

Satan rheumatism

Satan acute interstitial nephritis

Satan Lyme disease

Satan alcohol allergy

Satan drooling

Satan swine flu

Satan cholelithiasis

Satan genetic Parkinson's

Satan cholera

Satan pelvic organ prolapse

Satan aortic dissection

INDEX

Printed in the United States
By Bookmasters